PRAISE FO

MW00712204

"Not too many walk the walk and talk the talk. **Ash** is a pioneer of daily motivation. His words inspire me and my listeners daily."
–Egypt Sherrod, *Host of HGTV's Property Virgins*

"Ash Cash is a motivator and a voice that cannot be ignored. Through his Daily Words of Inspiration he helps many people, including my self, overcome many obstacles. Believe it or not, his words have helped change my outlook on life. "
–Jermaine Dupri, *Grammy Award Winning Song Writer and Producer, CEO of So So Def, Owner of Global14.com*

"Ash's words motivate people from all different walks of life. They reach across cultures, ages, genders, and races. His messages are truly inspirational."
– Derrick McDaniel, *JD, MBA, PMP, NYU Business Professor, Entrepreneur*

"**Ash Cash** is our generation's Les Brown. His words of wisdom have great impact and his delivery is powerful. In these times of uncertainty he is definitely a voice you can lean on."
-DJ Kut, *Music Director & Radio Personality at Radio One Broadcasting, Personality at KPLR-TV Channel 11*

"**Ash Cash** represents the clarity and genuineness needed to help move people forward. His advice provides a clear plan to help anyone serious about changing their life to become better."
-Jermaine "Jay Everyday" Smith, Radio Host, Fragrance Creator, Publisher, Producer and Award winning Playwright,

"**Ash Cash** gives profound insight into the intricate details of life. His practical wisdom serves as effective instruction on how to get from where you are in life to where you want to be."
-Yolanda Moore, *Two-time WNBA champion, Author of "You Will Win, If You Don't Quit"*

Second Printing: January 2015
Published by:
1 Brick Publishing A division of
Ash Cash Enterprises, LLC
P.O. 2717
New York, NY 10027-2717
(877)853-0493

Email: Info@1BrickPublishing.com;
Website: www.1BrickPublishing.com

Copyright © 20012 by Ash'Cash

All rights reserved. No part of this book may be used, reproduced or transmitted in any form or by any means, electronic or mechanical, including photocopying and recording, or by any information storage or retrieval system, without written permission from the publisher, except by a reviewer who wishes to quote brief excerpts in connection with a review in a newspaper, magazine, or electronic publication. Request for permission should be addressed in writing to:
Ash Cash Enterprises, LLC, P.O. Box 2717, New York, NY 10027

Library of Congress Cataloging-in-Publication Data
Cash, Ash, 1980-
Taylor's Way: Life Lessons Through the Eyes of a Three Year Old
By Ash Cash

p. cm.
ISBN 978-0-983-44862-4 paperback edition
Library of Congress Control Number:
Success I. Title II. Cash, Ash
Self-Help/Self-Improvement
Happiness
How to Succeed
Printed in the United States of America

This book is dedicated to my daughter Taylor. Thank you for showing me what life is all about

TABLE OF CONTENTS

FOREWORD
FIND YOUR INNER-CHILD..1

INTRODUCTION
FOLLOW YOUR CHILD'S LEAD..5

LESSON I
START EACH DAY WITH ENTHUSIASM.......................11

LESSON II
LIVE SPONTANEOUSLY..19

LESSON III
CREATE YOUR OWN REALITY.......................................29

LESSON IV
LEARN BY EXAMPLE..35

LESSON V
AIM NOT FOR PERFECTION..43

LESSON VI
FIGURE IT OUT & DO IT YOUR WAY............................51

LESSON VII
LAUGH & MOVE ON..57

LESSON VIII
TAKE FULL ADVANTAGE OF YOUR MISTAKES....63

LESSON IX
DON'T LET LACK OF QUALIFICATIONS STOP YOU..75

LESSON X
ASK LOTS OF QUESTIONS..............................85

LESSON XI
GET OUT OF YOUR COMFORT ZONE.................91

LESSONXII
EXPRESS YOUR FEELINGS..........................99

LESSON XIII
BE HONEST AND CALL IT LIKE IT IS.................107

LESSON XIV
ENJOY LIFE'S SIMPLE PLEASURES..................115

LESSON XV
NURTURE & VALUE YOUR RELATIONSHIPS........123

BONUS LESSON...131

EPILOGUE...133

ABOUT THE AUTHOR.....................................135

Note from the Co-Author

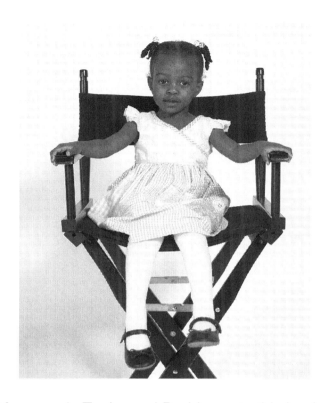

Hi, My name is Taylor and Daddy wrote this book because he said I taught him some lessons about life. Hopefully as you read it, you will see that kids are sometimes right. We may be new to the world but we can still teach a thing or two. I hope you enjoy the book and if so please let Mommy and Daddy know that there is nothing wrong with eating ice cream for dinner… for some reason they won't budge.
-Taylor Janaya (TJ)

- FOREWORD -

"You will find more happiness growing down than up."
–Unknown

As adults we have the tendency to blow most things out of proportion, making life more complicated than it really is. Whether we are parents or not, watching children maneuver through life will give us better insight on how to keep it simple and be happy. Taking a glimpse at a child's natural state of being can help us learn how to love, gain confidence and possess a drive that will assist us in reaching all of our goals and aspirations.

While its natural to want to groom, guide and protect children early in their existence, it is imperative that we allow them to be their genuine selves. Not whom they think we want them to be, or what society says they should be; instead allow them to find their own voice (which most will use to scream at the top of their lungs!)

1

Doing this will allow us to receive the lessons designated for us to learn; the most important one being don't sweat the small stuff and realizing that it's all small stuff.

Taylor Janaya (TJ); my greatest work to date has in three short years been one of the greatest attributes to my own personal and spiritual development. She has proven to be a constant confirmation of all of my thoughts (buried too far in the back of my brain for my liking) on how life should be lived!

It may sound cliché but Taylor is truly an angel sent specifically to help strengthen and guide our family! Life has changed for the best and she deserves most of the credit. I know, sounds like big shoes for such a small person to fill but I suggest you stop if only for a moment, open your mind and observe children without dictation. I guarantee you will see so many precious jewels revealed that you had not noticed before.

Taylor's Way is a book comprised of the very lessons my husband and I learned by allowing Taylor to be Taylor. Buckle up your seatbelt, grab some popcorn and enjoy the ride. ☺

- Taylor's Mom

(ALL PHOTOS COURTESY OF BERMAN FENELUS)

- Introduction -

"While we try to teach our children all about life, our children teach us what life is all about."
~Angela Schwindt

The next time you're around a group of children take a few minutes to observe how they play, interact and conduct themselves throughout the day. You will notice they are enthusiastic, always eager to learn, curious, brave and will try almost anything without hesitation. "They look with wonder at that which is before them" as Florence Scovel Shinn so eloquently stated in her book "*The Game of Life and How to Play It*". Children are continually in a state of joy and wonder believing anything can happen in the snap of a finger or overnight. When you think about it children know more about living a happy life than adults do and if we just pay more attention we can learn some valuable lessons.

Unbeknownst to me, the day my daughter was born

marked the beginning of a series of hands on real life lessons I would be taught about life and how it should really be lived. I knew being a first time parent was a learning experience but who knew my daughter would grow to teach me things that I thought I already knew. Just like my parents, their parents and all parents before; we believe that because of our experiences we can teach our children all about life. This was my intention and because my upbringing wasn't all flowers and roses, I believed it was my duty to shield Taylor from harm and prevent her from making the "mistakes" I made in my teenage years. Note the quotes around the word mistakes; I've learned since becoming a parent that those so called mistakes develop character and are just a part of life but I digress, we will get into more depth in later chapters regarding that matter.

I grew up in a single-parent home where my mom worked tirelessly to provide food and a roof over our family's head leaving her little time to nurture my brother, sister and I. While I am forever grateful for what my mother sacrificed for us, I always wished she didn't have to work so hard so that she could've been a bigger influence in our lives. Despite being a Haitian immigrant who knew little English and never attended high school, my mom did her best with what she had. I often had thoughts about how life would be if we had both parents in the household but I now know that everything happens for a reason and your past is what shapes your future. I was raised by the streets and worked in some shape, form, or fashion since I was nine years old. I did things at twelve that no kid had business doing and in my mind I reached adulthood by seventeen. I was sexually active very early, shot my first gun before puberty, got kicked out of school four times, and barely graduated from high school. In hindsight I realize how a strong family structure could have prevented all of that, but again all of those experiences are why I am who I am today.

Given my upbringing, I made myself a promise that when I do become a parent I would do everything in my power to nurture my kids and teach them how life works. My main goal was to purely make sure that they would not have to go through what I went through, leaving them ample time to just be kids. I knew it all!! I saw the good, the bad, the ugly and I figured out the magic formula to good living! The rude awakening came when I realized that all I thought I knew about life was really inaccurate.

For a long time what most people, including myself did was adjust themselves to a life that was altered based on circumstance and false beliefs; so in essence we were trying to find the right way to live a wrong life. We were told that the key to life was the American Dream; go to school, get an education, obtain a good paying job, buy a house, a car, and live happily ever after. Somewhere in that message money became the most important thing. Money seemed to make us happy and it essentially provided us with everything we needed in life. We didn't mind working 60-80 hours a week and not having time to spend with our family and friends because if we didn't work we wouldn't eat! We also didn't mind working at a job that we hated because again we had to do what we had to do in order to feed our family and ourselves. What's wrong about this message is that working long hours, doing a job that you really don't like, and not spending enough time with the ones you love are all ways that will ensure that you are never happy. What keeps us going is the hope that one day it will change. It gives us satisfaction that all the things we are sacrificing now will come later and it will all be worth it. The sad truth is 1) Tomorrow isn't promised to anyone and 2) If we keep waiting until later to enjoy life we will miss the best part.

I once watched a video on Youtube by Alan Watts called Music and Life. The video essentially compares music to life and explains how in music you don't make the end of the composition the point of the composition. It draws the accurate notion that when you listen to a composition, it's the entire body of work that makes it great, unlike life, where we are led to believe that we must struggle and work hard until we get to this end result; whether it is success, riches, retirement, or heaven. The point of the video was that we must treat life more like music! Don't wait until the end to enjoy it; sing, dance, and celebrate as life is playing. This is what children know; they understand key principles about life that we as adults try with every ounce of our beings to "correct." I put correct in quotations because as I watch Taylor I realize that she and every other child that has not yet been tainted, has the key to life!

In the following pages you will read all about these lessons and if you truly take heed you will live life the way it was intended for you to live! As you read remember that Life is abundant! Life is enjoyable! Life is exactly how you imagined it in your wildest dreams! Today is the day that you bring life back to that essence. Welcome to Taylor's Way: Life Lessons Through the Eyes of a Three Year Old.

- Lesson 1 -
Start Each Day with Enthusiasm

Every day is a new day! Leave the past behind and know that what's done is done and what is to come is none of your business. If you make the best of today every single day, then tomorrow will take care of itself.

"STOP ACTING AS IF LIFE IS A
REHEARSAL. LIVE THIS DAY AS IF IT
WERE YOUR LAST. THE PAST IS OVER
AND GONE. THE FUTURE IS NOT
GUARANTEED."
-WAYNE DYER

I've always been a big proponent of the power of thought! I believe wholeheartedly that everyone's life whether good or bad is a direct result of his or her thoughts. As adults we go through so many things and have so many experiences that it becomes difficult (or so we think) to put the past behind us. Kids on the other hand start each day with enthusiasm. They hit the ground running and have no memory of what happened yesterday and even if they do remember they do not hold on to it for very long. They are excited to be alive and look forward to the new experiences that lie ahead. This is the first lesson I learned from Taylor.

My wife and I have been together for more than nine years. What started out as a bet between a co-worker and me ended up becoming one of the strongest friendships and partnerships that exist in the world today. Sure you're thinking this is simply my opinion but if you saw us in action you would undoubtedly think the same. My wife and I are soul mates; with all of my craziness and of course with all of hers we still manage to be inseparable like macaroni and cheese, rice and beans, milk and cookies and all the other delicious paired foods you can think of (You can tell I love to eat :)). I'm telling you about our relationship because it was not always this way; she was my first serious relationship so I made many "my first relationship" mistakes. Thank God she was patient because sometimes I wondered how she put up with me, but I know now it was all part of the divine plan. Don't get me wrong, I never cheated, I wasn't abusive, nor did I do anything that could've landed me on the Maury show but understanding who we both were will give you better insight.

She was an only child, so like many only children she suffered from OCS commonly known as "Only Child Syndrome"; everything revolved around her and if it didn't there was a problem. Me, I was the youngest child so in turn I was a mama's boy a/k/a mama spoiled me rotten, I could do no wrong and it was my world and my way. The mixture of the two personalities was dangerous; we both expected to be catered to and that's where most of our early relationship problems stemmed from. As time went on we would argue about things that we now know were small and insignificant but it would last for weeks. I liked to argue and she didn't. I felt that we should deal with problems as they arose she wanted to wait until emotions were down. Her rational was that if we tackled problems as they arose we would be emotional and it wouldn't lead to a solution; it would just make things worse.... she had a point but I was just stubborn. Eventually we just adapted to each other and made it work. If we argued, we knew that we would be mad at each other for at least a week but eventually everything would go back to the way it was. This was the norm but by the time Taylor was born and got older she taught us different.

Taylor at three had fully developed her personality. It was a strong mixture between my wife and me. She was loud, outgoing, and played too much like me but reserved, smart, and defied authority like my wife. She was very determined and ALWAYS got what she wanted. She mentally could not process the word no and really didn't understand what it meant. Often times my wife and I would call ourselves disciplining Taylor for essentially challenging something that we said but most often it ended in Taylor getting her way. Being first time parents we sort of treated Taylor like a friend and because of this she often lobbied for equal rights. If it was bedtime for her, but my wife or I wanted to stay up, she would refuse to go to bed unless we all went together! Taylor loves to read so eventually my wife would have to bribe her with a bedtime story in order for us to stay up later. Usually if she pushed us far enough we would punish her by putting her on time out or taking away something she liked. When this happened she would cry and yell at the top of her lungs going to bed with the worst attitude. Despite the fact that she went to bed upset with us, she would wake up the next day as if nothing happened the night before. She woke up excited, enthusiastic, and was ready to take on the world.

Pulling from my adult experience, I expected her to wake up with the same attitude she went to sleep with, assuming that she would get over it as the day progressed. Nope!! Not Taylor! Everyday was a new day. Whatever happened yesterday was yesterday and today is today. She made sure she concentrated on the thing that was most in her control! TODAY!!!

Living life this way will allow you to fully take advantage of what it has to offer. Waking up each day with the intention to make it the best day of your life will ensure that life will be the best it can possibly be, what's done is done and to harp on yesterday will take away from what you can enjoy today. Live life on purpose and never let what you cannot control stop you from living your best life. As Jay-Z once said "Life is for Living, Not living uptight."

Next time you catch yourself being upset at someone, something, or some circumstance, remind yourself that there is absolutely nothing you can do to change the past. Things happen in your life not to make you bitter but to make you better. Realize what lesson life is trying to teach you then do everything today to show life you have learned the lesson. Start the day with enthusiasm!!! You only have one life to live! Live it Great!

- Lesson II -
Live Spontaneously

It is important to have a plan and know where you are going but when life gives you new direction, it is imperative that you follow wherever it may lead. Those who fail to plan, plan to fail and those who fail to bend are bound to break.

"STAY COMMITTED TO YOUR DECISIONS, BUT STAY FLEXIBLE IN YOUR APPROACH." – TOM ROBBINS

All of my life I've been a rule breaker! In my younger years it got me in trouble, later in life it made me successful. Despite this I always had some type of plan and followed it no matter what. I always lived by the notion that you should make as much mistakes as early as possible so that you can know what not to do going forward. This logic made sense but I realized that sometimes if you become too stubborn and unwilling to be flexible, you will find yourself going through some unnecessary hardships.

Right before I turned 30, I made a decision that I would leave Corporate America for good and become an entrepreneur. It was all or nothing and if I recall correctly "I Quit!!" were the two words that I brazenly walked into my boss's office and said. I had no reservations, just walked in and did what I had to do! True Story... Maybe it didn't exactly go that way. The truth is I was nervous! I contemplated for months, deliberated for weeks, and couldn't sleep for days. I drove my wife crazy asking her what she thought I should do. When it was time to go into that office and talk to my boss, my mouth was moving but my conscious mind was screaming "Ash!! What are you doing!!?" Despite my reservations I was convinced that it was time to take that "leap of faith", give myself to the world and become this undeniable leading expert in personal finances, Emmy award winning television host, and most sought after motivational speaker. I did my time in corporate America! 11 long years! We had the good, the bad, the highs and lows but my soul had spoken! It said, "Ash, you are great but in order for you to fully maximize your potential I need you to do me a favor" I said "What?" Soul said, "I need you to kill your day job!" "Huh????" Not just quit but Kill it! Walk away! Never look back and spend 150% of your energy building, maintaining, and sustaining your brand! This seemed illogical, unrealistic, crazy and risky but for some reason it felt right. I had a passion for teaching financial literacy, and wanted to motivate and inspire people with my story. With what I was feeling and all the signs that were being thrown my way, there was no doubt in my mind that it was now the time.

It started in 2009 with me just releasing my first book *Mind Right, Money Right: 10 Laws of Financial Freedom*. During that time, I began to receive a lot of attention from many media outlets; I was on Radio, TV, magazines and websites. Schools and conferences started booking me and my email-marketing list had grown to over 10,000 members. I was getting emails daily from readers who said I had helped them get through difficult times with my inspirational Daily Word blog. Needless to say I was becoming popular and my ego convinced me that I didn't need my 9-5. In my mind I was living a double life; I was just 24 hours away from greatness so why should I continue to be a slave to the clock when I can make $100,000 a speech like former President Clinton! Yup! I compared myself to President Clinton!! As time went on my bank account started to dwindle and reality started to set in; I began to realize that fame doesn't always equal money! In fact, while my bank account was on the steady decline my popularity was rising making it more and more difficult for me to do what I ought to do... which was go back to work and allow the paycheck to fund the passion. See the original plan was that I would promote my book as much as possible and make enough money to meet my basic obligations; I would then hire a booking agent or join a speaking bureau to get me booked at different colleges, conferences and organizations. At that point, my popularity would soar and I would land a television and/or radio show that would increase my notoriety. I would hire a manager who was already well connected, who would bring me other cross-promotional and business opportunities making me a very wealthy man. This plan was worth more than $1Million dollars and it would all happen within the first two years. Obviously none of this happened, well not entirely... I did sell a lot of books in fact one week I was ranked #7 on Amazon.com for personal finance books. I did hire a booking agent, joined a speaking bureau and found a manager. The problem was that none of these things brought in enough money to sustain my family and my lifestyle as I thought it would.

Before I left the bank I was making six figures but now I was making about half that. As I chased this dream, I watched as my 6-8 months of emergency funds diminished to almost nothing; my credit score started to take a beating because I could not meet all of my obligations and my wife and I almost lost our home because there wasn't enough money coming in to sustain it. I had many opportunities to stop the bleeding but again my ego wouldn't let me. Through out the journey many opportunities arose to go back into the workforce but I declined them all because of my stubbornness to follow my plan. Each time an opportunity came up I thought I was being tricked. I saw it as a test from my higher power to see how committed I was to achieving my dream instead of looking at it as a blessing. In the best selling book "The Secret" by Rhonda Burnes, it says that "You get to choose what you want, however, how it will happen is not your concern or job. Allow the Universe to do it for you". This quote resonated with me because that was exactly my problem, I knew the WHAT but was too stuck on the HOW and because of this I delayed what I knew the universe had in store for me, which was the easiest, quickest way to my desired success.

The realization came in while watching my daughter Taylor. No matter what, she always got what she wanted. She rarely planned anything and just lived life as it happened. She was spontaneous and took advantage of every moment for all it was worth. Obviously as a three year old, her wants were very basic; have fun, eat junk food, and go to the movies. Because of her age one can say "Of course, she takes life as it comes she's 3, she has no choice" but the truth is that at any age if you are spontaneous enough and willing to go with the flow, life can become so much easier.

An example of this is Taylor's craving for Pizza. Pizza is her favorite food and given the opportunity she would have it for breakfast, lunch, snack, and dinner. Every opportunity she gets to have Pizza she will take. If she specifically asks to go to the Pizza shop and is declined she will attempt again and again until her wish is fulfilled. The spontaneity comes in at the fact that she doesn't mind if she gets the pizza from the pizza shop, the supermarket, pizza hut express, Wal-Mart, or any other place that can fulfill her need.

This is exactly how life should be! Lets say the Pizza represents your dreams and aspirations and based on your experience you believe that a Pizza shop is the only place you can get Pizza from. You set yourself on your journey and your eyes are only on the Pizza shop. As life continues to happen you're so stuck on getting the Pizza (Your Dreams and Aspirations) the way you have planned it, that you have closed your mind to all the other ways that you can reach your end result.

Live life spontaneously! These days there are many places you can go to get a slice of Pizza! Know exactly what you want, know how you plan to get it but don't be so stuck on YOUR way that it blinds you from the many opportunities that life has to offer. The universe is abundant! By understanding this fact and living life accordingly, you will find your bliss and live your best possible life! Always remember that the World is Yours! The only thing that can stop you is YOU!!

- Lesson III -
Create Your Own Reality

Your imagination is the pathway to what you can have in the future. Let it run wild and you in turn become the creator of your own destiny. Those who believe that reality is only what they see right now, lose out on the possibilities that life has to offer. Thoughts truly become things.

"THERE IS A FINE LINE BETWEEN DREAMS AND REALITY; IT'S UP TO YOU TO DRAW IT."
-B. QUILLIAM

The phrase "be realistic" has to be one of the most crippling, destructive, demoralizing and dream killing phrases ever put together! Those two words have probably killed more dreams than a million alarm clocks going off at six in the morning after a three-day weekend. Being realistic makes an assumption that there is only one reality and has people interpreting someone else's experience as the absolute way of life.

So far in my short time on earth I've had many dreams and aspirations; from wanting to be a lawyer, to hopes of being an actor, and aspiration to going to the NBA. All of these dreams never came to fruition because for some reason or another (mainly because I was being "realistic") I allowed them to die and dissipate. Most of my life I believed that I needed guidance when attempting something I knew nothing about, so in doing so I always reached out to the people

I most trust. This group of individuals consisted of mainly family and friends and because their experiences were limited, so was their advice.

When it comes to family and friends the phrase "I'm not sure, let me find out" doesn't really exist. Because of their obligation to be there when needed, some rather give wrong advice than no advice at all. In all honesty, I know the intention comes from the right place but this can be very damaging to say the least. When inaccurate advice is given, what you wind up having is the blind leading the blind, which also leads to many dreams being deferred or completely discarded due to discouragement. You'll here things like "you're too old", "that's impossible", "why would you want to do that" and of course "be realistic." When I was trying to get to the NBA I consulted folks who knew nothing about the ins and out of getting to the league, while wanting to practice law my counsel came from people who had no clue about what it took to be a lawyer, and while aspiring to be an actor the only advice that was given was that it was very competitive and nearly impossible to make a living from. Because of my dependency on a helping hand, I took this advice and made it my reality. Instead of allowing my imagination to run wild, I created limitations that stopped me from giving my absolute best and then found excuses to justify giving up. I do strongly believe than you can learn from everyone, no matter the age, gender, experience, or circumstance but the key is to not allow other peoples opinion to become your truth. Listening to others stumps your imagination and only gives you access to what reality says at the moment. Opinions are not fact but unfortunately many people treat them as such.

Taylor on the other hand and most kids for that matter truly do not digest opinions like adults do. Their imagination will always override your reality and in doing so they remain open to what life can really offer. Even if you tell a kid something repeatedly the odds of them accepting your truth are slim to none. They are whatever they say they are and nothing can change that (until they get older, of course). Kids use their imagination to discover new things about themselves as well as the world around them. They believe in the many things that we call impossible and somehow create it as their reality, even if it's only for a short while.

We should never allow our imagination to grow dormant. It is in our imagination that our dreams and our curiosity to chase them are developed. If we begin to replace our imagination for what popular belief calls reality then we will never see our dreams through to the end. Impossible is what people call things when they haven't found the solution, genius is what they call you once you do. Let your imagination run wild and become the genius that you are. Reality is what ever you say it is!

- Lesson IV -
Learn by Example

Anything that you want to do has been done before. If you are willing to take heed to the many examples set before you, it will help you along your journey. Whether good or bad, these examples can teach you valuable lessons that will assist you in reaching your goals.

*"LEARN FROM THE SUCCESSES &
MISTAKES OF OTHERS, YOU WON'T LIVE
LONG ENOUGH TO MAKE THEM ALL
YOURSELF!"
-UNKNOWN*

Many studies have shown that children develop the most within their first years of life. According to Texas Children's Pediatrics, "The experiences during a child's first 3 years determine the permanent 'wiring' of the brain." Because of this it is important that parents pay close attention to what they say and do around their children.

Taylor is a sponge with excellent memory; she imitates phrases, facial expressions, body language, voice tone and whatever else she believes will get her what she wants out of life. On the many occasions that my wife and I are having an intellectual debate, you will almost always observe Taylor watching attentively as if it were a brand new special feature Disney film. As soon as she is finished soaking up whatever she's observing, she will then mimic her findings to determine what works and what doesn't. I remember one time catching her in the mirror practicing crying which I believe was the starting point of her figuring out, that as a child "crying does pay."

From birth to about two years old Taylor was a rather quiet kid. She wasn't much for putting up fits and was pretty well behaved. Right before she turned two, a series of events would happen that would change how Taylor got what she wanted as well as become the catalyst for a valuable life lesson. Up until that point my mother was Taylor's sole babysitter. They had a great relationship and acted like old friends. My mom, who is a type II diabetic with many health issues, suffered a stroke that would permanently alter the way she functioned. As a result we immediately put Taylor into a school/day-care paying a little over $300 a week for what we thought would make our lives easier. Instead, this move would not only cost us a lot of money but also expose Taylor to other kids who had this life thing down pat. Within a month of her attendance she all of a sudden started to become a chameleon. If she wanted something and couldn't get it, she began to whine and cry without letting up until her demands were met. This was sudden and took us by surprise being that it was a habit that was unusual for her.

The correlation between her whining and school didn't come together until I witnessed with my own eyes the melee in which the inmates where running the asylum. Like clockwork, child after child would cry and the teachers would pick them up, baby them and give them what they wanted. I realized that Taylor was simply learning by example. She was surrounded by kids who used the tactic of crying and throwing fits to get what they wanted in a blink of an eye. Eventually as my wife and I caught on, Taylor had a rude awakening when the tactic didn't work anymore. But the more she observed other kids the more she became a master of disguise. Eventually she became a different person depending on whose company she was in; she realized what buttons to push to get what she wanted by observing how people interacted with each other. As I continued to observe Taylor and how she functioned, the lesson became clearer and clearer.

As adults we become brainwashed with this notion that we must find our true selves and once we find it we must never compromise or deviate from that person. The problem with that notion is three fold. First, if you keep doing what you've always done you will continue to get what you've always gotten. Second, the idea of finding a true self somewhat implies that we are predisposed to be a certain way but with no prior knowledge of this predisposition how would we ever know when we truly arrived? Lastly, finding a true self or being who we are robs us from life itself because life is growth and growth is change. The only place that it is acceptable for someone to be the same day in and day out is in the cemetery.

Prior to understanding this lesson from Taylor, I was of similar mind that tried to stick to the core of who I thought I was. I was stubborn and wanted to do everything my way. In going after my dreams and aspirations, I always took the trial and error approach convincing myself that my own experience was the best teacher in all cases. What needs to be realized sooner rather than later is that anything we want in life has probably in some shape form or fashion been done already. Instead of always trying to re-invent the wheel it is important that we become more observant and learn by example. It is true that experience is the best teacher but it doesn't always have to necessarily be ours. Other people's experience can cut down our learning curve and get us to our goals or aspirations faster. We must stop living in a box and only believing in the way we've always did things. Find someone who is already achieving similar success to what you want to achieve and begin to follow his or her lead. At our core we do have values and characteristics that make us who we are and learning by example doesn't mean you stop following those values or characteristics to become someone else. It simply means that you can save yourself time and get to your bliss faster by adapting your style to what already works.

Life will never be about finding yourself! As the creator of your destiny you hold the pen that writes the script to your life. If something isn't necessarily going your way, at any moment you have the power to change it in your favor! Create yourself. Observe everything around you, realize what works and disregard anything that doesn't. It is impossible to live long enough to make all the mistakes yourself so you might as well live, learn, and benefit from those that have already been made. Learn by Example! This will be the best class you ever attend!

- Lesson V -
Aim Not For Perfection

Those who wait for all conditions to be just right to start something new will rarely start anything at all. Give yourself room to make mistakes and learn from them whenever they occur. Begin now where you stand and adjust along the way.

*"SOMETIMES... WHEN YOU HOLD OUT FOR
EVERYTHING, YOU WALK AWAY
WITH NOTHING."
-ALLY MCBEAL*

Growing up I was always told that I wasn't going to amount to anything. This was mainly because I was so much of a disruptive and defiant kid that it was hard for anyone to fathom that my fate would be anything other than death or incarceration. These prophecies that people dictated as my destiny made me very self-conscious and critical about what I did on a day-to-day basis. As you read these words they may seem to have a nonchalant tone to them but believe me, at one point repeating that many people prayed for my demise enraged me. Now that I understand life a little better I realize how most people draw their conclusions.

Human beings as a whole are very critical and pessimistic people. We are more likely to believe that something negative will happen than positive even if logic tells us otherwise. In most situations we expect the worse and hope for the best. We aren't born that way but as we grow older and deal with other people's cynicism we begin to adapt this destructive trait.

Our pessimism is so prevalent that all it takes is someone to fail once or twice in order to stop trying something even if they succeeded at the same thing many times before. It's mainly because we care too much about what other people think and worry what they will say about us if we fail. We know that people are always extra critical so in our subconscious we prepare for that and are always on the defensive.

And to our critical nature we can credit the simple theory that says, "Hurt people hurt people." The cycle of throwing stones even though our own house is made of glass continues and we breed a society of people who accept criticism as a way of life.

All of this pessimism and criticism turns into hesitation and fear and makes most people afraid to try something new unless their plan is perfect. Their fear of being crucified makes the thought of making a mistake unbearable and forces people to avoid them at all cost.

In 2004 I took my first sabbatical from Corporate America. I was a private banker managing the accounts of the mass affluent clientele (net worth of $250K and greater). Working with this population exposed me to the fact that I was an entrepreneur at heart. Many of my clients owned businesses and built them from humble beginnings to semi conglomerates.

My biggest client at the time was an immigrant man who started a small retail shop in 1975 in the south Bronx, catering to the fashion needs of a growing hip-hop generation. By 2004, the shop had grown into a chain of 11 stores in the New York City Metro area at the same time my client's net worth grew to $22mm.

Having access to people like that gave me the gall to say, "If they can do it, so can I". When I quit banking in 2004 my plan was to start a business management firm catering specifically to the finance needs of those in the music business. Through other side ventures, I had pretty decent access to those in entertainment so I figured this would be a great way to turn my access into a paycheck.

When it was time to quit I was impulsive. Being someone that is stubborn it is very rare that I can be talked out of doing something I set my mind to. My plan was set and I was ready to go. The problem was that once I took the leap I tried to make my plan so perfect that I ended up never even starting the business. I took some odd jobs to supplement my income but returned back to banking within 8 months. My fear of failure was so great that even with everything on the line I couldn't convince myself to simply get going. Every time I was ready I found another excuse to prolong starting my new venture. The habit of hesitation and fear was in full swing and it literally paralyzed me.

Taylor, who is one of the bravest souls I know, has never allowed herself to be stopped by hesitation or fear. She is always ready to jump head first into every situation, leaping over hurdles and adjusting her approach when she has to. When presented with an obstacle she shoots first and asks questions last.

I remember the day that Taylor graduated from the baby park with seesaws and baby swings to the big park with wall climbing and monkey bars. She went from slides that were maybe four feet high to the swirly ones that stood about ten. The first time she slid down there wasn't a nervousness in her eye. She watched as the big kids slid, hands straight out and head first in what they called the superman. Most landed just fine however when it was her turn she must have miscalculated the speed in which she would be going and hit the ground scrapping her face just a tad. Normally for adults or older kids that would be it, but like a trooper she dusted herself off and tried again. This time she learned that the superman thing might not work so when she slid, she went leg first, extending them like scissors to brace herself just in case she fell. As I continued to watch her, I noticed that each time she took a turn she was just as excited as the first. No hesitation, no fear. Eventually as she started to venture over to the wall climbing and monkey bars it was my parental warning telling her "Be careful princess", "Make sure you hold on tight", "Don't hurt yourself" unconsciously instilling fear and hesitation.

We sometimes try to protect our kids but by exposing them to potential dangers we may be stifling them and making them fearful of things that might not happen. We over-analyze most of our next moves and hesitate in fear that we may fail or not get it right.

Like Taylor and most kids who are not scared straight, we need to understand that the chances of getting it right 100% the first time is slim to none. We must always be ready to deal with the mistakes, bumps, bruises and disappointments along the way and do what we have to do to get it better the next time. Practice makes perfect but if you never start then you'll never learn.

Next time you have an idea, dream or aspiration, plan your course of action and know how you want to achieve it. Do so with the understanding that your plan doesn't have to be perfect and it will most likely change many times. Begin as soon as you can and keep your eyes on the prize. Use your momentum to keep you focused, and map out the details as they come over the horizon. A perfect plan is a plan that is tried, tested, and adjusted along the way. You don't have to be great to start but you must start in order to be great!!

- LESSON VI -
Figure it Out and
Do it Your Way

When available, learning by
example and conventional wisdom
are great ways to navigate
through life but solely relying on
these methods can be the setup for
a setback. Use your ability to
analyze a situation to allow you to
come up with new and innovative
ways to solve life's problems.

"Obstacles don't have to stop you.
If you run into a wall, don't turn
around and give up. Figure out how
to climb it, go through it, or work
around it."
-Michael Jordan

As I stated earlier my wife is an only child, so like most only children she suffers from "Only Child Syndrome" or OCS, as we will now call it. OCS is a condition where a parent has only one child and spoils that child so rotten that he/she grows up being the center of attention and gets use to always getting things their way. They find it difficult to comprehend concepts like sharing, waiting or being part of a team. Common side effects include impatience, defiance, a sense of entitlement, total independence and lack of respect for authority.

In the beginning I started to see signs of OCS in Taylor. If she wanted something it had to be done NOW or she would keep asking until you got annoyed enough to just give her what she wanted. As she turned three she stopped the "non-stop asking until she gets" scheme and simply would ask once and if you didn't comply fast enough she would figure out a way to get it herself. This somewhat upset me at times because on occasion her independence required her to climb up high chairs risking her getting hurt.

Despite this one nuance, I secretly admired this attitude because it signaled to me that she would grow to be a go-getter if the attitude stayed in tact. One day in particular bought a smile to my face; we were in Chuck E, Cheeses at my niece's birthday party and we had just gotten to the part where the kids hit the piñata. Mind you these are three and four year olds so each time a kid took a turn the parents tried to assist. Some of the kids, including Taylor would not allow anyone to help them.

Child after Child swung the baby bat trying to be the hero who supplied their peers with endless candy, but kid after kid left disappointed when the piñata didn't burst. Parents yelling "swing it faster", "swing it down", "swing it up", "you almost got it Nay Nay", "put more power to it"... All the while everyone is getting frustrated because the piñata isn't seeming to break. Not until one of the kids hit it and saw a little bit of light by way of a small hole in the bottom of the piñata. Now parents are screaming "we almost there", "Just swing a little harder", "you got it baby", "I know you can do it".

When it was Taylor's turn she was holding the bat upside down, looking at the piñata as if she was analyzing it. With all the adrenaline pumping through the parents, instructions on how to hit the pinata were coming from everywhere. "Turn it upside down" "go baby go" "hold it with two hands". Taylor stands underneath the piñata, looks around annoyed by the unwanted assistance and begins poking the hole in the bottom of piñata with the other side of the bat until it gets stuck. With simply pulling the bat out of the piñata, it burst's and Taylor becomes the hero. All of the parents look at each other in somewhat confusion but began to cheer once the kids start to hit the ground to collect their riches. In that instant I inwardly rejoiced as my daughter defied conventional wisdom and won! For years "hit the piñata" was only played one way, now by simply being innovative a new and more effective way was discovered.

Anthony Robbins; one of my heroes and mentors, once said "Create a vision and never let the environment, other people's beliefs, or the limits of what has been done in the past shape your decisions. Ignore conventional wisdom." Taylor learned this lesson early and now as you read these words, realize how significant that statement is; just because things have been done the same way for many years doesn't mean that you should continue to do them that way. Sometimes conventional wisdom works but other times you are going to have to do things your way and uncover new and improved methods to reach your goals.

Next time you have an innovative and creative idea about how to accomplish something faster, smarter or better than the current way, do it your way and see what happens. The worst thing that can happen is that you learn from your mistake. It took Thomas Edison 10,001 tries to invent the light bulb and as he said "I didn't fail 10,000 times, I just found 10,000 ways that didn't work." Keep going until!!!!!

- Lesson VII -
Laugh and Move On

When things are going wrong don't go with them. Never allow what may seem like a big deal stop you from getting on with your life. No matter how bad the situation, laugh and move on. The number one rule in life is "Don't sweat the small stuff" the second rule, "its all small stuff"

"WHEN LIFE GIVES YOU LEMONS INSTEAD OF COMPLAINING ABOUT HOW SOUR LEMONS ARE, ADD SUGAR AND MAKE LEMONADE."
-UNKNOWN

As adults we take life waaaay too seriously. If we set out on a plan and for whatever reasons that plan doesn't go accordingly, we act like it is the end of the world. When kids are presented with unexpected obstacles they usually laugh it off and work around the problems. I remember my wife and I planning to take Taylor to go see Yo Gabba Gabba live at Radio City Music Hall. Schedule conflicts, work deadlines and other setbacks had us putting a hold on many family outings but we finally had a date and were ready to go. DJ Lance and the Yo Gabba Gabba crew would only be in town for a week so the timing couldn't have been better. This was Taylor's favorite show so she was excited and eager with anticipation. The day of the show was horrible; nothing was going according to plan. It was a rainy stormy Sunday and the mood was just gloom. Traffic was backed up and we're running late because my wife decides to change her clothes like 10 times as if we're going to a fashion show. I'm aggravated; Taylor's making noise in the car, and my wife keeps trying to engage me in conversation because I obviously look annoyed.

We finally get to the venue and the lobby is packed like you don't know what! We waited on line for almost an hour and by the time we get to the ticket booth we were told that we couldn't get in. Murphy's Law was in full effect (Anything that can go wrong, will go wrong). Apparently when I ordered the tickets I asked for them to be mailed to my P.O. Box and like a genius I never went to pick them up. Assuming that the venue had a more sophisticated system, I thought that by showing my email confirmation receipt they would be able to manually check us in..... WRONG!!! Each ticket had its own unique number and they needed it to assure no duplication in seating. Not only did I waste $350 on tickets (We had great seats), $48 for parking (We were in the heart of midtown), and God knows how much in gas (We were traveling from Westchester County in our gas guzzling SUV) but I also manage to ruin my daughters chances of seeing her favorite folks in the world. I was distraught, embarrassed, and disappointed in myself. I put my head down in shame, as I looked my daughter in her bright brown eyes to tell her Daddy messed up. To my surprise Taylor shrugged it off. With a big grin on her face she looked up and said "Daddy, its ok". I don't know if she was feeding off of my energy of defeat but in that instance she pumped me back to life by giving me a good ol' fashion unsolicited leg hug.

My wife and I now accepting our fate looked at each other and without saying a word we knew that we had to make it right. My daughter kicked into full gear as a participant of this conflict resolution. She made many suggestions of things we can do and by the fourth suggestion we had our alternative. We wind up going to my sisters house.

My niece Kay Kay and Taylor are like best friends. Only two months apart but they have a twin sibling bond that seems unbreakable. It was a Sunday so my sister was cooking that good ol "Sunday after church food" so for the next four hours we had the time of our lives. The girls were playing and having fun, my wife and sister were talking about whatever woman talk about, and me and my brother-in-law were chopping up sports and throwing back some cold ones (Well I don't drink so I had ice cold lemonade). This was the type of fun you couldn't pay for. It was a relief to go from the end of the world to the beginning of bliss all in a matter of minutes. With a change in perspective and collective problem resolution, we were able to find an inexpensive way to solve a seemingly insolvable problem.

This would not be the first nor the last time we would deal with some unexpected obstacles but the more I watched how Taylor handled disappointment, the better I understood how it was suppose to go. No matter how much you plan, no matter how much you prepare, there will always be some things that we just can't anticipate. Life will always throw you some curve balls but it is in how you deal with those curve balls that will determine your success or failure.

Laugh and move on! Even when it seems like you are in the worse possible situation you must remember that you're not. The worst thing that can happen is death! As long as you have breathe in your body you will always have an opportunity to make it right and do it better. Next time you're in a jam, remind yourself that it isn't the end of the world. You will have as many chances as you decide to take. Decide not to ever be crippled by life's circumstances. Move on and make great things happen! Nothing can stand in your way unless you let it.

- Lesson VIII -
Take Full Advantage
of Your Mistakes

Some mistakes may seem like the
end of the world but if you change
your perspective you will realize
how much a blunder can turn into a
great opportunity. When mistakes
happen, take time to learn from
them and use the experience as a
stepping-stone for something
greater.

"THE MAN WHO MAKES NO MISTAKES DOES NOT USUALLY MAKE ANYTHING".
-EDWARD PHELPS

When I decided to leave Corporate America the second time around I knew it was the opportune situation. Every sign was pointing me in that direction and every ounce of my being was telling me that this was it. We were in the worst economic time since the great depression and people were loosing jobs left and right. Many people with advanced degrees had to settle for minimum wage positions so of course leaving a six-figure job with one degree in finance was the best decision to make (I'm being facetious). Despite logic telling me I was crazy and asking me how I was going to pay the mortgage or maintain my family's lifestyle, I still knew that I had to make it happen.

After I made the decision I regretted it for weeks. Asking myself day after day what did I do? As the bills started to mount I started to question my decision more. I dubbed this the biggest mistake I've ever made. How can someone so smart be so dumb!!! My passion was financial literacy and I ran a bank!! How did I possibly think that this position wouldn't give me the leverage I needed to fulfill my passion? My questioning started to become doubt and my doubt eventually became self-consciousness. Here I am traveling the country, speaking at major conferences and universities, telling people what to do with their money all the while trying to figure out how I can make more to survive. It wasn't like I didn't know what I was talking about. In fact, being in the business so long I've helped countless people change their mind set about money and become more responsible. I even helped set up savings and investment strategies that put some of my client's kids through college. Now my temporary setback had me doubting something that I actually had a successful track record doing.

Externally I was fine; I always had a smile on my face, I kept great energy and always had a positive can-do attitude. But internally I was a mess; I questioned most of my moves, battled with self-worth, and desperately began to have a dependency on money. As I started to reflect on my decision, I realized that it was indeed ego not intuition that allowed me to walk away from a somewhat perfect situation. As I thought of different ways to right my wrongs it became more and more difficult to face my mistake. One day, down to my last few dollars, I had a moment that would change how I looked at my situation and taught me how mistakes really affect life.

Basketball, for a long time has been my biggest stress reliever. No matter what is going on at any given moment if you give me a ball and some kicks I can clear my mind. Every Saturday like a ritual I drive up to Dobbs Ferry, NY to play some games of pick up. The sports club I frequent comes equipped with a basketball court, pool, sauna, cycling area, and yes a play area for young children. Taylor usually accompanies me to the gym and while I play ball she's in the play area with the other children for the allotted two hours.

On this particular day when it was time to pick her up, her and the other children were competing to see who can build the tallest Lego block the fastest. As soon as Taylor notices me she starts smiling from ear to ear. From the looks of things she's winning and to share this moment with the best dad in the world is an added bonus (her words, not mine.... Well... That's what she was thinking I know it).

Suddenly her Lego block starts to wobble and just in that instance the tallest structure was no more. Apparently her building did not have a solid foundation; she simply piled one block on top of the next. The higher she built the structure the more unstable it became. By the time I walked in she had clearly won but I guess she was trying to show off so she kept piling block on top of block. Ultimately the structure couldn't hold anymore and tumbled down. Just like that, Taylor went from 1st to last place. The winner for the day ended up being another young lady whose Lego block wasn't as tall as Taylor's but had a foundation of four to five blocks, making the base very sturdy and not susceptible to crashing down.

As Taylor surveyed the room looking at how the others manage not to have their Lego blocks tumble, she notice that most of them started at the bottom, created a strong foundation and built themselves up. The whole ride back Taylor had this look on her face that I couldn't tell whether it was disappointment or just her thinking face.

When we reached back home without saying a word to anybody, she went upstairs to her room pulled out her Lego's and went to work. Build, build, build.... Crash!!!

Build, build, build.... Crash!!! Build, build, build....
Crash!!! This was the scene for most of the night until
she figured out what the other kids had already known.
If you place one Lego on top of the other the base
wouldn't be strong enough but if you did three or four on
top of each other it would be sturdy. As night progressed
she started to experiment on building three to four
blocks as the foundation for maybe four or five steps
then going back to one block so she can be the tallest...
Eureka!!! She got it!!!!

The next trip to the gym she became the victor! The
other kids kept their same strategy of creating a
structure with three to four blocks each row. Taylor did
that for the first five rows then went to two blocks, then
to one. By the time she was done, her structure was
reminiscent of the empire state building. By simply
learning from her mistake (not building a foundation) she
was able to test and retry her new approach in a bigger
and better way. She could have easily allowed the
previous mistake to defeat her but by not letting the
mistake do so; she got what she wanted.... Sweet
victory and baby bragging rights!!

In life this is how children differ from adults. Kids
don't beat themselves up when they make a stupid

mistake; they examine their error and figure out how to come back stronger. After learning this lesson, I decided that I wouldn't allow my mistake to cripple or stop me from living out my purpose. Instead of being down and out about my current situation, I instead used my smarts, recognition, good looks ;) and experience to land me a few writing gigs to increase my visibility, a few contracts teaching financial literacy, and more television and radio coverage. This positioning began to open doors and many opportunities. The one in particular was one that would come full circle.

I decided that I would re-release my book, change the cover and put my face on it like the Suze Orman's, Dave Ramsey's, and Robert Kiyosaki's that came before me. I would embark on a massive promotional campaign attacking the streets, radio, Internet, and magazines. I held many free events where I would speak about the principles that were in the book and gave priceless advice for a fraction of the cost.

On one rainy evening I spoke at the Hueman Bookstore in Harlem, NY to a packed standing room only audience. The conversation was great, the audience was attentive and the vibe was just right. One of the audience members, Edwin, a friend of mine who actually use to be my boss way back when I first started working, had never seen me in action. After the talk he was amazed at my ability to motivate and inspire the crowd (his words for real this time). Edwin worked at a major financial institution and word had just come down from up top that they needed to do more community outreach. He began working on getting me a contract with his bank to go around to their branches and give financial workshops.

Red tape and personnel changes didn't allow the contract to happen but nonetheless my work was introduced to the higher ups of the company and now they knew my name and what I did. I continued to do my thing; traveling from state to state spreading the word of fiscal responsibility, when one day I got a call from Edwin stating that one of the branches in my hometown was without a manager and needed someone to run it. He had mentioned my name as a possible candidate and immediately the higher ups where eager to make it happen.

At first my ego said "nah you can't go back to banking" but my true intuition said that this was the best situation at the best time. Not only would I be making more money than in my previous position, I would also have to do many financial workshops in the community because this branch was in a Business Development District (BDD) and participated in a state funded program that provided funds to the bank to give out loans with a contingency of doing community outreach.

This was me having my cake and eating it too. Not only would I now become a Vice President at one of the largest financial institution in the world, providing financial literacy to an under served community, and making money to do it, I also would be given a bigger opportunity than before to push my passion forward.

I interviewed and got the position within a week. It was exactly what I expected and more. It immediately gave me more credibility than before and opened doors that I couldn't open as an independent.... I'm talking board of director appointments to major non-profits, and meeting with respected politicians and dignitaries that wouldn't exist as simply Ash Cash! Now that my name was attached to a major financial institution my calls where returned within the hour.

Taylor's lesson of learning from your mistakes put me in the perfect place at the perfect time. Instead of beating myself up about the dumb mistake I made, I got myself together put myself out there and now took myself forward five steps in the quest for spreading financial freedom and economic development. The fact that my ego allowed me to make a big mistake, helped open the door for a greater opportunity. If I had never quit my job to go on my own, I would have never been discovered for this opportunity of a lifetime.

I now know for sure that making mistakes is usually what opens the door for new experiences and growth opportunity. When things don't go according to plan you need to use what you learned to help you get further. Those who don't make mistakes don't take enough risk and if you don't take risk then you aren't really pushing your limits. Don't be afraid to make mistakes and understand that mistakes aren't the end of the world; learn from them and give it another shot until you get what you came for. It's always too early to quit! If you understand this fact then you will learn the key to fulfillment and happiness. Life is about perspective.... no matter what; always look on the bright side.

- Lesson IX -
Never Let a Lack of Qualifications Stop You

Those who think they can and those who think they can't are both right. Never stop your quest for greatness merely because of a lack of qualifications. You'll be surprised at what you can accomplish by simply making an effort. Take advantage of every opportunity that you are afforded.

"WE ARE ALL FACED WITH A SERIES OF GREAT OPPORTUNITIES BRILLIANTLY DISGUISED AS IMPOSSIBLE SITUATIONS."
—CHARLES R. SWINDOLL

I'm fortunate to be married to a woman who is as caring, supportive, and equally ambitious as me. Our relationship is a great balance between lovers, friends and confidants. Without her unwavering support many of the risk I took in life (which lead to many successes) would've probably never happened. Anytime I had a new idea she was behind me 1000%. If I woke up one day and said I wanted to be a professional clown (I'm already a clown on my leisure time) she would probably dust off the red nose and polish the shoes. She is what we call a "Ride or Die Chick", a woman that will stand behind her man no matter the circumstance. When we were abundant with money, we were abundant together; when we started to struggle, we struggled together; when it was time to make sacrifices, then it was time to make sacrifices. This type of support within a relationship rarely exists, so to be able to experience it at such an early age is something I would never take for granted.

Her support for me was so strong that sometimes I thought she believed in me more than I did myself (Which is almost impossible because I have a strong belief system). If I had an idea that I wanted to pursue and felt I didn't necessarily have the qualifications for, she would argue with me saying that I must not wait and just do it. In my mind I would think, "that's easy for you to say because you're not the one who has to take the risk" but later on Taylor would reinforce this message and set me off on a journey towards greatness.

If I were to rank myself as a professional speaker I would say I rank among the top 10%. I'm articulate, funny, personable, and I own the stage whenever I'm on it. When I first started my speaking career I was only comfortable speaking in small crowds. As I got more seasoned, I dreamed of attacking bigger venues but my nervousness would lie and tell me that I wasn't ready. I began to pick up speaker trade magazines and join speaking groups to get over the fright. As I read more and continued to participate in my groups, the fear got worse. Apparently these different outlets were convincing me that without the proper experience and speaker credentials I shouldn't embarrass myself because it takes a lot to be ready for the big stage.

That was it!! These were the professionals who have done this for years telling me that I needed more skills, so they had to be right! Eventually my fear led me to turning down a few keynote speaker gigs because I knew the crowds would be large. My wife would yell at me and say, "People are people!! If you can talk to one you can talk to a thousand!!" When I would attempt to give her the excuse about needing speaking credentials or more experience she would comeback with the line about experience being the best teacher. She was right but I still had my fears. The funny thing was that this was the advice I typically gave to others and now I couldn't practice what I preached.

Even though I knew the advice to be true, I began to be taught examples by watching Taylor. In everything she did she was never concerned with her lack of qualifications. If it was her first time trying something, she was even more eager to jump in the water head first. If she didn't succeed the first time, she would brush herself off and try again until she got it right.

Her first time riding a bike was exactly this way. She had never rode a bike before but jumped on like she knew what she was doing! Despite not even knowing how to pedal, she leaned forward and pushed with her body as if the bike would just start. She fell a couple of times but like a trooper she just got back on and eventually she got it.

But the real lesson would come from not only Taylor but from a group of Taylor's peers; three year olds who had no care in the world and not a hesitation bone in their bodies. It was the end of the school year and the whole pre-k class was participating for the first time in the schools annual production. Their part was a brief rendition of "oh holy night". The crowd was packed with students, faculty, and parents. When it was time for the show, the pre-k's stormed on the stage bright eyed, happy, and ready to make it happen. As their teacher prepared them, they looked out to an attentive crowd put their hands by their sides and began to sang! Most of the kids were off cue but the chaos was organized. You can tell that they practiced hard and by the end of their performance you had a proud crowd who were delighted at this group's tenacity and courage to stand up on the stage and pour their hearts out. This was a group who just learned how to say complete sentences and here they were in front of a crowd of 100-200 people singing an orchestrated production.

Seeing their fearlessness inspired me. Not only were they "unqualified" to be on that stage but they had every reason to be frightened. Despite that, they did all they can do to be ready and took on the opportunity the best way they knew how. That rule of needing qualifications didn't apply on this night and nor did ASCAP, BMI or any other association of singing professionals have a problem with these three year olds who wanted to sing.

In all honestly, sometimes qualifications are just man-made restrictions created by those who want to keep passionate newcomers with great ideas "in their place". We've seen it with book publishing, music, television, photography you name the profession and I guarantee that there are people who are imposing limitations; claiming that new comers are ruining the business. Don't get me wrong I'm not saying that any pre-med student should just pick up a knife and do surgery or am I saying that there aren't any great organizations out there that help develop talent. What I am saying is that in some instances that voice that is telling you that you are not qualified to do something (whether the voice is internal or external) can be absolutely wrong!

The first time I finally got on the stage in front of a crowd of a thousand or more I did great! I won't lie and say that I wasn't frightened, but remembering the courage of Taylor and the gang gave me the courage I needed to do what I had to do. Eventually large crowds became a norm and just as my wife stated, "people are people." I realized that the fear of not starting based on lack of skill or qualification was a bogus fear! It wasn't based on anything substantial and was a self-imposed limitation. In fact I had already spoken in hundreds of places prior to my large gig but I guess the fact that I was now getting paid convinced me that I would be less dynamic. Logically it made absolutely no sense! This situation confirmed that fear is a habitual liar; the biggest offender known to man. By allowing that fear to dominate, I almost gave up an opportunity to do what I know I've been put on this earth to do; inspire and motivate.

Next time you are given an opportunity to do something in life, never be discouraged by a false sense of feeling unqualified. You know more than you think you know! You can do more than you give yourself credit for! If you continue to doubt your abilities then the life you will lead will be a life filled with mediocrity! If you begin to trust yourself and go confidently where you know you should go, then your possibilities become endless!! Always strive to put your best foot forward but don't use excuses as a way to justify procrastination. Your greatness awaits! Do what you have to do to make great things happen!! The only thing that can stop you is You!!

- Lesson X -
Ask Lots of Questions

He who asks a question is a fool for five minutes; he who does not ask remains a fool forever. Asking questions is the easiest way to find the answers to life's problems. The solutions will always be within your reach if you are willing to dig deep enough. Never lose an opportunity to learn how to make life better. You are always a question or two away.

"At the end of the day, the questions we ask of ourselves determine the type of people that we will become."
-Leo Babauta

- Lesson XI -
Get Out of Your Comfort Zone

In order to get what we want out of life, you must be willing to make the sacrifice and get out of the rut of normalcy. Where you are right now is nowhere near where your potential can take you. By staying complacent you close the door to all that life has to offer. Everyday you must be willing to grow and maximize your full potential. Be better than you are right now!

"LIFE BEGINS AT THE END OF YOUR COMFORT ZONE."
-NEALE DONALD WALSCH

It is said that a child's brain develops the most between the ages of three and five. This is such a crucial moment because most neurological growth (the growth of brain cells and cognitive thinking) takes place during this time. To put it simply your child is like a sponge; it soaks up all information that it is given and stays open to receiving more.

This ability that children have to absorb information keeps the child's mind open to all the world has to offer. Because they haven't yet been tainted by life, most of their judgment is based on what they've witnessed and little is influenced by outside sources. They are eager to try something new and excited to see new outcomes. This is another key to happiness and a great way to get what you want out of life.

As embarrassing as this is to say, I do not know

how to swim. In fact as a man who stands at six feet; three inches, I am petrified of any water above four feet. My first time trying to swim was when I was about thirteen years old. One of my close friends knew I had a fear of water so just like friends would do; he plotted with some other folks to grab me and throw me in the water.

Because those who had bad experiences swimming had already influenced me, my expectations were purely negative. When they threw me in the water I nearly killed myself. I had a closed mind and no one could convince me otherwise that swimming wasn't dangerous. Even when logic told me that it wasn't, my emotions and anxiety took over and created a semi-panic attack. I was not trying to learn anything new and even though they threw me in the shallow area, my mind told me I was going to die.

As I flapped and screamed (Yup, I was screaming) trying to save my life, all I can hear is my friends saying "Stand up! Just stand up!!" After about 30 seconds of putting on a fit, one of the young ladies that was at the pool, jumped in and helped me to my feet; this was one of the most embarrassing times in my youth. I realize now that I was so stuck in my comfort zone that when I was taken out of it, I didn't allow my mind to adjust itself to what I knew instinctively.

Taylor on the other hand didn't have this problem; she was somewhat a natural swimmer. When my wife took her to swim for the first time it was almost as if she had done it before. She was three years old and at that pivotal time where she was observing, absorbing, and eager to learn new things, so convincing her to give swimming a try was easy to say the least.

She watched as my wife and other swimmers use their hands and feet to glide across the water and also noticed how many of them where able to float at times. By the time it was Taylor's turn, my wife assisted but in no time she needed no one. She jumped in the water (life vest strapped tight) made some simple mistakes but was able to flap her little feet to get from one side to the other.

This is just one example but there are many illustrations that show how a child's open mind gives them courage to always be ready to try something new. As we hit adulthood, instead of having that same instinctive zeal, we become creatures of habit and stay confined within our comfort zone. If something doesn't look familiar we shy away from it and tend to force ourselves back into familiar territory.

What we need to realize is that when we close our minds and stay only within our comfort zone we are also closing our life to the many opportunities and experiences that life has to offer. We live in a universe that is abundant but in order to take advantage of this abundance you must be willing and able to go where the universe guides you. You are insane if you keep doing the same things and expect different results; this isn't me being mean or malicious but just stating the facts.

Mary Mary an American gospel music duo, consisting of sisters Erica Atkins-Campbell and Trecina "Tina" Atkins-Campbell have an inspirational song called "Go Get It." In the song, one of the sisters is heard saying.... "It's alright to crawl before you walk, it's alright to walk before you run, but if you wanna get what you never got, gotta do something that you never done". This line resonates with me every-time I hear it because it's the absolute truth!

As I said before, if you keep doing what you've always done, you'll keep getting what you've always gotten! The only way to live the life you truly want to live is to get comfortable being uncomfortable! Stop Thinking and Living in the Box! The box is simply about mediocrity and robs many people of the joy that they deserve and are entitled to!! Get out of that box and live beyond in the land of the extraordinary. Don't be afraid of discomfort. As author T.Harv Eker once said: "Nobody ever died of discomfort, yet living in the name of comfort has killed more ideas, opportunities, actions, and growth than everything else combined."

Next time you are confronted with an opportunity or experience that seems frightening because it's out of your comfort zone, stop and think about the possibilities you are potentially giving up. Then stop and think about the worst thing that can happen and realize that it really isn't that bad. Right now as you read these words understand that a better and exciting life is waiting for you and you simply have to keep an open mind in order to receive it. There will be many people who will try to distract and deter you based on their experiences but again realize that this is your life to live so you might as well live it the best. Keeping an open mind is about taking chances; it's about seeking the good out of every opportunity and not being afraid of the unknown. Life is adventure!! Get out of your zone and make life exciting!!

- Lesson XII -
Express Your Feelings

It is important to never conceal how you truly feel on the inside or out. In order to fully experience happiness you must be free to be yourself with no restrictions. Hiding your feelings takes away from who you really are and moves you away from true bliss.

"Be who you are and say what you feel because those who mind don't matter and those who matter don't mind."
—Dr. Seuss

Disclaimer: I am not a scientist nor am I in any way equipped to discuss biological concepts. In fact through out my whole academic career I was a "C" student as it related to science. Nonetheless I do understand the theory of "Survival of the fittest." It is a phrase originally coined by British philosopher Herbert Spencer who was explaining the evolutionary theory as an alternative description of natural selection (A theory by Charles Darwin). It's simply a term used to describe how living things evolve and adapt to changes in the environment. These changes make species able or more fit to survive in a new element or environment. (Google for a more detailed explanation). Today, the phrase is not used in its original context. In this day and age "Survival of the fittest" is how people look at everyday life. Its no longer about change in environment, it's about only the strong surviving in every environment.

With this way of looking at life, the world becomes a place filled with scarcity mentality. People believe that there isn't enough for everybody, so they hold tight to everything that comes their way. Instead of people working hard, to the best of their ability, to get what they deserve from life, they are concentrating on what the next person is doing and in turn treating life like a competition. It becomes a place where every man is for himself and where dog eats dog. We see crabs in a barrel, who are so afraid to lose out on life, that they hate anyone with ambition and try their best to take people down.

This competitive view of life makes people defensive, deceptive, and non-trusting. They wear masks daily; afraid of being who they really are, because of the fear of being taken advantage of. Many people want to be their kind, trusting and loving selves but somewhere along the line they were taught that their emotions could be used against them.

We watch this daily as people hurt inside and instead of seeking help they continue to hurt until they eventually self-destruct. Or how about the people who belittle their happy moments and accomplishments because they are afraid to let their light shine. Trying to figure out what an adult is feeling sometimes becomes rocket science and is more difficult to figure out then a trigonometry problem on an aptitude test.

My wife who was born to a teenage mother was not only raised by her mother, but by her grandmother, aunts, and uncles as well. Being the first niece and granddaughter afforded her many advantages and queen like treatment at an early age. Her family was very protective of her so they did everything in their power to shield her from the "real world." Her uncles did an excellent job of teaching her the tricks of the trade and how most men try to run game (Thanks Uncles!! Lol!). These advance lessons proved problematic for me in the beginning because anything I did with sincerity was viewed with a skeptic eye. Not only where my actions being scrutinized but I also didn't get to know who my wife really was early on, because she hid her emotions and never revealed how she truly felt. This caused major communication blocks and misunderstandings that could've been the demise of our relationship. Fortunately we got to know each other better and realized that none of us were the enemy. This message became clearer with Taylor.

Taylor wears her emotions on her sleeves. You don't ever have to guess how she's feeling because all you simply have to do is look at her and you'll know. Whether she's happy, sad, angry or indifferent, her facial expression and body language tells the whole story. As parents this gives us an advantage because we can easily trace the root cause of an issue and realize how to continue or stop a certain behavior. This is advantageous to Taylor as well; because she feels what she feels and doesn't apologize for it, she is free to be herself. She doesn't live a lie or have to keep up a facade. This way of living gives us peace of mind and allows our brain to concentrate on the more important things in life.

As adults it is imperative that we stop concealing our feelings from others. We need to stop making it so difficult for people to figure out how we feel. By expressing our feelings openly it makes communication easier and maintains honest relationships. I've seen friendship go on for years where one party despises the next but for some reason hides it and still maintains the relationship.

A happy life is one that is honest, transparent, and free from judgment. It is one that doesn't have room for compromise but instead accepts and appreciates how others feel and expects the same in return. I'm not saying that everyone deserves a front row seat into your life but those who you choose to share with, should not be left in the dark. As Dr. Seuss once said... "Be who you are and say what you feel, because those who mind don't matter and those who matter don't mind. Express your feelings! Let the real you shine brighter than you've ever shined before.

- Lesson XIII -
Be Honest and
Call It Like It Is

Relationships should be built on honesty, trust and transparency. Never compromise the truth in order to spare feelings. Be tactful in your delivery but never rob someone of the opportunity to grow. No matter how uncomfortable, the truth will always set us free.

*"THOSE WHO THINK IT IS PERMISSIBLE TO
TELL WHITE LIES SOON
GROW COLOR-BLIND."*
~AUSTIN O'MALLEY

It is often said that I am too diplomatic. Not because of my political views but because of my constant need to spare people's feelings and for being non-confrontational. I call it simply being tactful! I was told early on to treat people, as you want to be treated so this lesson stuck with me and I took it to heart. Many times if I can help someone save face, I would do so with no hesitation because I believe that there are easier ways to let someone down. If something is asked of me that I can't or won't do, instead of being rude or abrasive I find the nice way to say no.

Eventually this diplomatic way of doing things morphed itself into telling little white lies. You know the type where someone asks whether they look fat and instead of saying yes or no you answer with "you look good!" Or being invited to a function that isn't going so well but when asked you say that the event is going great! Soon enough I started to care so much about people's feelings that I began to compromise my own, to make other people happy. I would attend things that I didn't really want to attend, cancel plans to accommodate others, and simply put other people's needs ahead of mine. They say never take kindness for weakness but that was exactly what was happening to me. My kindness became my weakness and I began to find myself in uncomfortable situations.

I soon became such a people pleaser that I lost sight of the damage that I was doing to others and myself. As a person who has always been the underdog, I always tried to find the good in what people were doing so that I can inspire and motivate them to keep going. My intentions were always good but by omitting opportunities for others to do better I began to hurt folks more than I was helping.

When you tell people what they want to hear or do things that you really don't want to do or support, not only are you not being true to who you are and what you believe in but you are also taking away their ability to become better and guaranteeing that they stay stagnate and not grow. I'm not saying that your opinion of others is law but holding back what you really believe, takes away people's right to reflect on perception. No matter how you feel people will react to what you say, if you really care about a relationship, it is in your and their best interest that you tell them the truth. If you feel a particular way about what someone is doing, then the odds are maybe others feel the same. Giving up that knowledge allows people to access what they're doing and change if they see fit.

Besides being a businesswoman and writer, my wife is also a cosmetologist that sometimes has to attend to clients on the weekends. Normally the weekend is the time that She, Taylor, and I spend together and on Saturday mornings she usually fixes us homemade breakfast. Our favorite dish is fried fish and cheese grits with a tall glass of orange juice. On this particular Saturday, as my wife was at the shop, Taylor says to me "Daddy, I'm hungry! I want some fish and grits." As a "mamas boy" there were many things I never did for myself and cooking was one of them. Nonetheless, I never shied away from an opportunity to learn something new so I gave it a shot. I know what you're thinking... "Fish and Grits? How difficult can that be?" And that was my thoughts exactly!

As I tried to fix my baby girl some breakfast and

remember exactly how my wife usually prepared it, I all of a sudden got this burst of confidence that said, "This food is going to be awesome." I remember my wife using just salt and pepper to season the grits but as a fan of Sa-son, I figured I'd used that instead. If you're not familiar with Sa-son, it's an orange seasoning powder that is usually used to season meats. As you can imagine the grits turned orange instead of its usual white grainy look. When I was done, the fish was slightly burned or crispy as I like to call it and the grits were chunky and orange, but smelled great.

As I fixed Taylor's plate, I noticed a strange look on her face as she looked at the food. Immediately while looking at the grits she says "ill!!! What's that?" She picks up the fish, pokes it with her fork, looks at me and says... "I don't want it!" What!!!!!!!! Do you believe that she wouldn't even taste it!! Not one bite!! I was furious but this taught me a valuable lesson.

As I stated earlier, kids don't hide their feelings and they wear their emotions on their sleeves. They are honest to a fault and are rarely tactful about how they say things. They call it like they see it, as it happens, with no compromise or regard to feelings. I realized that Taylor's refusal to eat my food had more to do with her lack of compromise then it did with how she thought it would make me feel. She was expecting something different and when it didn't meet her standards she decided that she would not just lower her bar to appease me but would hold steadfast on what she believed. Even though she did miss out on some awesome food because she judged a book by its cover. (The Sa-son was an excellent touch) The lesson was loud and clear be honest and call it how you see it.

Being honest and communicating clearly builds better relationships than trying to spare people's feelings. When you speak the truth, some people might not necessarily appreciate you at first but eventually they will respect you. It shows strong character and in the long run helps move relationships forward.

When I first started working in corporate America, I had a manager named Michael Black, who once told me very frankly to stop talking as if I was still a homeboy from the neighborhood. He told me that I should learn how to articulate my words better and to stop wearing such baggy clothes.

At first I was disturbed by his candor but until this day, I credit him for many of the successes I've attained thus far. It was his honesty that made me buy grammar books to learn the English language better. It was his frankness that got me started reading the wall street journal and New York Times to learn how to have better economic and business conversations. His being direct even led me to buy audio CD's that helped with my vocabulary and GQ magazines to learn how to dress better. Without the initial constructive criticism a lot of who I am today would probably not exist. The point is simply that sometimes the truth hurts but it is necessary in order to create progress.

I must confess that I am still today very much diplomatic; the only difference is that I will not compromise myself, my integrity, or the truth for the sake of sparing feelings. This has built my character and has allowed me to become a trusted advisor to many. I still don't condone rudeness or being abrasive but being honest is a non-negotiable item.

Next time you are put into a situation where being honest may hurt someone's feelings remember what long-term damage you'll cause by not doing so. I don't advise that you are as honest as Taylor was, but there's always a tactful way to tell the truth, the whole truth, nothing but the truth, so help you God!

- Lesson XIV -
Enjoy Life's Simple Pleasures

The best things in life are free. Take every opportunity to enjoy life's simple pleasures and never let lack of money or time be an excuse to live a mundane life. Life is an adventure if you decide to make it so. Let nature guide you and live life to the fullest.

"LIFE IS REALLY SIMPLE, BUT WE INSIST ON MAKING IT COMPLICATED."
-CONFUCIUS

One of the biggest myths that has ever been told is that money equals happiness. Millions, maybe billions of people go around everyday believing this lie and in turn spend their whole life chasing money. The truth is that money DOES NOT equal happiness. Yes it can buy the things that we think can make us happy but money itself is just a means to an end. In fact there are many people who by society's standards are considered poor who are the happiest people on earth. Conversely there are many people that have a lot of money who are stressed, depressed and miserable.

It is imperative that we get rid of our dependency on money ASAP! We should never get so consumed with the almighty dollar that we don't take time to enjoy the simple pleasures of life. Growing up I was a victim to this ideology of money equaling happiness. Because my family and I were relatively poor our access to those with money was limited to what we saw on TV and what the television (or Tell-Lie-Vision) showed was a strong correlation between the two. We never saw the ugly side, the substance abuse side, the side where people were so obsessed that they sacrificed friends, family, and significant others just to die alone with all of their money.

Naturally because I believed in the all-powerful money=happiness myth every attempt at having fun had to include spending money. If it was free or low cost then I was convinced that it couldn't possibly have adventure to it. In my mind I believed that the more expensive it was the more fun I would have. By the time I was old enough to date the young ladies, my idea of a great time was equivalent to how much money I spent.

This rang true when I first started dating my wife. At the time I was a 21-year-old personal banker making about $40,000 per year and still living at home, so my disposable income was plentiful. Our lavish habits included fine dining, Broadway plays, and the occasional weekend getaway. Eventually as we got deeper into our relationship and responsibilities started to grow, the lavish spending on fun stopped and was relegated to blockbuster video nights and takeout.

This is right around the time that our ambitions began to grow so we became homeowners and business owners, and most of our cash went into trying to maintain the two. We knew that we wanted to plan a family soon, so another priority was to save cash in order for us to be able to afford our first child. Needless to say our relationship became mundane. Like clockwork we did the same things over and over; worked, movies, takeout... Work, movie, takeout.... Work, movie.... (You get the point). My wife would suggest things to do like go to the park, the museum, and walking... Walking???? The Museum???? Are you kidding me! What fun is that? For a period, our relationship became so routine that it began to be no fun... We were like roommates who hardly saw each other because our work and business started to consume most of our lives. We justified this with the money=happiness myth. We said... "Its alright that we're not having fun and most of our friends are... Its the sacrifice we have to make in order to live a better life." Our rationale was simply that we would work the hardest we can right now and once we start making the money we would then take a step back to have fun and enjoy each other. Who were we kidding; this was a recipe for disaster.

By the time Taylor was born and old enough to converse, we noticed that what she considered as fun never had anything to do with money. She didn't need a room full of toys in order to have a great time, nor did we have to do any special events. She played pretend with the pillow, had fun with kitchen utensils, played in the rain or rolled around in the snow. Her version of fun was cheap, long lasting, and more enjoyable. It was these simple pleasures that gave us a different meaning to life.

My wife and I took full advantage of this. We used this as an opportunity to re ignite not only our inner child but the flames in our relationship as well. It felt like we took a swig from the fountain of youth because now as parents we became kids again. All of a sudden taking a walk was enjoyable, going to the beach to sit in the sun was part of our routine and sitting on the porch at night to count the stars was fun to do. We didn't require money to enjoy life; we took full advantage of each other. We enjoyed talks, game nights, laughing, playing around, and simply being childish. This worked wonders for our stress level and all around harmony in the household. We hardly had disagreements and dealt with obstacles as one cohesive unit.

The lesson and moral of the story is simple: Don't

find excuses as to why you cannot enjoy life today. Everything you need is in your possession right now. Some of the best things in life are free or are extremely low cost. Don't live above your means just for the sake of keeping up with the joneses or to impress people, instead realize that the simple things are unlimited and add joy and peace of mind to your life.

The next time you find your self in a rut, put everything down and take a walk. The moment you begin to feel that you are not doing enough and that life can be better, is the moment you need to take a step back to smell the roses you have right now. Be grateful and don't take for granted the many blessings that are currently at your disposal. It is imperative that you live life to the fullest anything else would be uncivilized.

- Lesson XV -
Nurture and Value Your Relationships

Never take for granted the people in your life who help give it meaning. People are in your life for a reason, season or lifetime. Identify who fits in each category and nurture those relationships as such.

"Never take someone for granted Hold every person close to your heart because you might wake up one day and realize that you've lost a diamond while you were too busy collecting stones."
—Rachel Ann Nunes

Some say too much is never enough but truth be told too much of anything can become a bad thing. Human beings by nature have addictive behaviors. Some are addicted to drugs, alcohol, gambling, fame, money, and even success. Like drugs, success induces a feeling of ecstasy that many quickly become addicted to and feel as if it's needed as part of their life. Again like drugs, once you get accustomed to that feeling of ecstasy you require a stronger dosage to continue to sustain. Most people believe that chasing greater success once you attain it, is about money or greed but its more than that; its about the feeling and rush one gets by topping their previous success. It's a high that is so addictive that people begin to not care about what they have to sacrifice in order to get to that next level.

Growing up I had a very small family. Most of my aunts and uncles were still back in Haiti so my family only consisted of my mom, brother, sister and I. My mom barely spoke English and with only an elementary school level education, the types of jobs she could get was very limited. For most of my mothers working career she worked in sewing factories making just above minimum wage. With no father in the household, you can imagine that living off of that kind of salary with three kids can be somewhat of a challenge. (Somewhat?? Nah it was definitely beyond challenging).

Because of this struggle, my siblings and me had to figure out how we could help out around the house at an early age. I always noticed that the kids who packed grocery bags at the supermarket always dressed better, had the best snacks, and if they were nice and smiled a lot had tip cups filled with dollars instead of coins. At nine years old I decided that this was how I would contribute to the household.

On average I would make about $17 per day which was more than enough for my mom to feed us because she knew how to make a dollar stretch. Eventually by twelve I outgrew packing bags and graduated to selling music cassette tapes and t-shirts in front of the Apollo theatre on 125th street. By seventeen I got my first real job working at Blockbuster Videos and by nineteen I became a banker. In every position I ever held I always excelled very quickly. While packing bags I went from the express lane to deliveries within months; as a street vendor I went from having my own table to managing a team of tables in a little under a year; at Blockbuster I went from customer service to assistant manager within six months and as a banker I went from bank teller to Vice president in just four years.

Most of my ambition started out as a promise I made myself to never have to struggle again but the deeper I got into my work I became obsessed with getting promoted. That obsession cost me a lot of friends but so what! I needed money and my friends were not putting any in my pockets! That was my thought process but eventually I wouldn't get the message until it was too late.

As I stated earlier, my mom suffered from a stroke that permanently altered the way she functioned. Prior to this happening my mom would constantly complain to me about her health almost daily but I was so consumed with work and success I kept brushing it off and not taking it seriously. Finally the last time she asked, she looked like she was really in pain so I set up a doctor's appointment to get her checked out. Her appointment was set for Wednesday... On Tuesday she had the stroke! I was devastated!! Even though I believe that everything happens for a reason, I got the message loud and clear! This was my first lady, my everything, the reason why I even had gotten this far but I still put her second to my thirst for success. This thirst was real and it allowed me to take advantage of many of my relationships. The higher I got, the more money I made, and the bigger the corporate title, the more I identified with my work. Instead of being Ash Cash, I became Vice President of such and such or Best-selling so and so.

This over-identification with work is one of the biggest reasons for the anxiety and depression that is running rampant in our society today. People are so afraid of losing their status, title or all of their worldly possession that they become mentally unstable and stress themselves out trying to sustain it.

After this devastating life changing event with my mom, I went through a period of blaming myself for her condition and fell into a slight depression. Surprisingly it was the same friends I neglected chasing success who were there when I needed them most. Friends like Marquise and Shawn who came to my rescue more than I can even count. Comrades like Jimmy and Derrick who never hesitated to be of assistance or Spiritual advisers like my friends Taqiy and Mike who always knew how to support me from a spiritual perspective. Of course my wife, my sister, and even my mother at her altered state continued to be my rock and biggest support system.

I now started to pay more attention to the things that mattered most. I told people I loved them more often, I made more time for family and friends (especially my mom) and even designated days in which I would do absolutely no work. My sister and I got closer; I began to make it my business to see her more often. In some of the many trips I made to her house, I always loved watching as Taylor and my niece played and had fun. They were thick as thieves. They laughed together, cried together, played together and ate together. If it were up to them, they would never leave each other's side.

In watching them, I realized more how kids admired, respected, and trust their friends and family unconditionally. They anticipated seeing them and never wanted to separate. They are aware of the benefits of healthy relationships and nurture them every moment they get.

Sir Winston Churchill once said "We make a living by what we get, we make a life by what we give." Make sure as life gets busier and responsibilities start to mount that we don't forget to give our time and love to the ones who matter most. We should never let success and our ambition keep us from the people we care about most. Tomorrow isn't promised to anyone so enjoy your loved ones before its too late.

Next time your life becomes so busy that you don't have time for anything or anyone else, take a step back and realize what is more valuable. Success will come and go but true friends and family will always be there!

Bonus
– Have Fun –

When putting this book together, having fun was the first lesson that came to mind. Often times as life got tough the first thing I did was try to put myself in a state of nostalgia and thought about those days when I had no care in the world. You know the days.... The days where playing was the first thing on the to do list.

As I watch my daughter daily I realize how much fun she is having and recognize that its time to go back to that essence. She is grateful for every moment and looks forward to that next moment where she can have even more fun. Playing comes naturally to her so her goal and purpose is to figure out how she can create more playtime.

For many reasons as we get older, life as an adult gets dull. We forget about our innate ability to be playful, so life becomes too serious. Everything seems to be about survival and anytime we go beyond surviving we feel guilty or believe it's too good to be true. We remain pessimistic about life so we expect it to go back to the day where it's all work and no play.

We know that this isn't the way life should be so

some of us begin to explore ways to mentally escape. When you look at alcohol, drug abusive, gambling, mental disorders, and even some infidelity, most of it is as a result of people attempting to run from some part of their current reality.

What we need to realize is that we can have our cake and eat it too. Life is the way it is because we have accepted that as the way. Yes there will be some struggle and strife and yes sometimes life may give us serious situations that require our full attention but its important to know that fun and laughter can be the answer to all of your troubles.

Thoughts become things and as you put your mind in a space of ease your thoughts begin to reflect how you feel. Feel good, then your thoughts become good, feel bad and your thoughts reflect that as well. This is the secret to a better life. Instead of running around stressed and worried about what we call the real world, remove yourself from the chaos and have some fun. The fun you have will be therapeutic and become the catalyst that will guide you towards your real bliss. Let loose! Play around! Do something crazy! Stop always looking for purpose behind your actions. Sometimes the healthiest thing you can do is fool around and have some fun.

EPILOGUE:

Thank you so much for taking the time to read Taylor's Way. My hopes is that the lessons and stories have inspired you to tap into your inner child and to live life the way it was intended for you to live. I also pray that this book provided you with a blueprint on how to start living a rich life now.

Napoleon Hill, (one of my favorite authors of all time) once wrote about the 12 true riches in life which include

A Positive mental attitude, Sound Physical Health, Harmony in human relations, Freedom from fear, Hope of future achievement, Capacity for applied faith, Willingness to shares ones blessings with others, To be engaged in a labor of love, An open mind on all subjects towards all people, Complete self-discipline, Wisdom with which to understand people and Financial security

Notice that money is the last thing that makes people rich. Continue to stay focused, keep your mind right, believe in your abilities and everything you ever wanted will be yours. As a matter of fact, everything you ever wanted is already yours!! Believe in this fact and make your life great!!!

ABOUT THE AUTHOR

Ash'Cash is a Personal Finance Expert, Author, Motivational Speaker, & Business Consultant with more than 10 years of banking experience. Widely recognized for his charisma, outgoing personality and his passion for financial literacy, Ash is on the forefront of a movement that is encouraging individuals to be socially and financially responsible. With his daily emails of inspiration regarding finance and life style change, which currently reaches millions of people daily, Ash challenges his readers to never quit and be the best that they can be. He is also a Husband, Son, Brother, Uncle, Best friend and by Taylor's accord, the Greatest Dad ever! For More Information on Ash'Cash Please Visit www.IamAshCash.com

WHAT ARE PEOPLE SAYING ABOUT ASH'CASH AND THE DAILY WORD?

"First thing in the morning is tricky. Through blurry, sleepy eyes, I prepare **AllHipHop.com** for the day's readers to enjoy - and the readers are tricky, too. We're connecting mostly young, minority men to the urban music and culture they love, while knowing that their emotional sides are often muted and uncared for. **Ash Cash** has found just the right combination of inspiration, swagger, and truth to tap into our readers' minds and hearts through his **Daily Word** column on the site. I feel better about the day knowing that **Ash** has fed our readers well. I feel better about myself knowing that his morning dose of sunshine is coming my way, too."
-Seandra Sims, *Editor-At-Large, AllHipHop.com*

"I can't start my day without reading **Ash'Cash's** "Daily Word". I am a positive person but sometimes I have my spots where I'm feeling a little down and its always at that time that **Ash** ends up touching a topic that resonates with me. People have cups of coffee and I have the "Daily Word". **Ash** is such a positive influence on this world and I wish there were more like him."
-Mike Success, *President/C.O.O of Trackateering Music*

"Being inspired on a daily basis via the **Ash Cash** "Daily Word" is priceless...From childhood Friends growing up in the projects to adulthood entrepreneurs **Ash Cash** is living proof that one is not a result of its environment."
-Rasheen "DaTaxGuy" Odom, *Founder/CEO DaTaxGuy LLC*

"I look forward to reading **Ash Cash's** Daily Word every morning. As an Entrepreneur you have to stay motivated and its refreshing to have such positive reinforcement that will inspire me to keep focused on the vision."
-**Jean Alerte**, *Entrepreneur, Author of Do Right, Do Good*

"I need my Daily Word like I need breathe in my body! The Daily Word helps me on a daily basis and I am not complete without it. **Ash Cash** is a godsend and his words help start my day on the right foot. Thanks to **Ash** I can also spread the positive messages to others."
-**Global Vito™**, Heavy Hitters, WQHT Hot 97.1/ 107.5 WBLS Producer

"**Ash Cash's** daily words of wisdom and motivation inspire me from the very start of the day. He's definitely a true leader and great asset to the entrepreneurial community."
-**Charles "BlaQ'smith" Smith**, *Entrepreneur; Owner and operator at Quality On Cue Music*

"Through **Ash Cash's** Daily Words of Wisdom, he has helped me to see that It is impossible to teach what you don't know, improbable to lead where you won't go, and unlikely to reap what you don't sow." As he says often "It's always too early to quit." I appreciate the impact his words have on my life
–Bill Bute, *Talent Development/Communication Trainer.*

"I belong to a World Peace organization and I forward **Ash Cash's** words of wisdom to various members. His words encourage my members and myself. I thank him dearly.
-**Elizabeth H**, *World Peace Organization*

"**Ash Cash** has contributed to the positive change in my life - there aren't enough words to explain the impact from his inspired words. The 'ME' today just reflects it."
–Charlene Thomas, *Marketing Executive*

137

"I used to spend many days/nights wondering what would be next in my life once I made the decision to quit my corporate job in 2010. With no real plan in sight, just the desire to learn myself & understand my passion, I embarked on a trying journey. However, I always looked for positive vibes & words of encouragement on a daily basis & I found it in **Ash Cash's** Daily Word. Lost with uncertainty but persistent in direction, I found that each day when I woke up w/ a question, The Daily Word had my answer. I am Forever grateful!!
-**Denisse Ocasio,** *writer/business owner*

"The Daily Word is truly a pick me up. **Ash Cash** and his words of wisdom help me think in ways I never had in the past and lets me know I'm not the only one in this world who needs morel advice on pushing thru life challenges, allures and bad thinking habits. **Ash**, thanks for keeping me on the straight and narrow and for pushing me to be a high achiever in life and better person with others."
-**Marquise Hardin**, *Boeing Air Craft Firefighter/EMT*

"**Ash Cash's** daily words help challenge me to be a better person. They make me think about what's important in life. They are also fun to read.
-**Roman Gbego-Tossa,** *Toronto student*

"**Ash Cash's** words have truly inspired me. They have gotten me through some tough times and also let me know what I can do differently in life. Because of him, I am taking control of my life and taking action to be financially free. Thank you!"
-**Jarvis Williams**, *Author of 10 Keys to Creating a Positive Work environment*

"**Ash Cash** always keeps me inspired! I do network marketing and its especially difficult to keep the team motivated and focused, but without fail his daily inspirations are right on point. "
-**Haywood Stokes**, *www.LogicMixx.Tumblr.com,* @haywoodStokes